How To Let Go and Let God

From Worldly Pain to Spiritual Freedom

Regina Baker

ACKNOWLEDGMENTS

To God be the Glory for the things HE has done. I thank you for being mindful of me, teaching, guiding, loving, and having the patience with me to fulfill Your will be done.

Thank you to my late husband, Ruben, for loving me like I've never known love.

Thank you to my Mom who loves me unconditionally and supports everything I do. I love you more than you could ever imagine!

To my siblings, Reginald, Roslyn and Rhonda, I love you all to Life for your constant love and support even when you don't have a clue what I'm doing.

To my mother-in-law, Mary, no matter what, you love me! Thank you for sincerely claiming me as your daughter, I love you!

To my best friends for life, Tami, Debra and Taffy. May God continue to bless you and your families. The support and patience you all have... who else would? {laughing}, I love you all to life!

I sincerely thank you all!

CONTENTS

FORWARD

Give it to God at the Altar and pick it back up as soon as you walk out the door of the Church! I tell you that would have been my constant theme if my life had been playing out over the screen many years ago. I am sure many of you know what I am talking about. You sincerely want to give it to GOD and yet, you think you should help him out along the way.

Believe me, Regina Baker has hit the nail on the head when she released *"How to Let go and Let God"*. She does not in any fashion come to you all puffed up or better than you, she is very humble and sincere in revealing what happened in her own life as she learned first hand *"How to Let Go and Let GOD"*. What she has so candidly written on the following pages will provide the practical tools that WILL make you take a look at yourself. Remember Michael Jackson's song that says *"I'm starting with that man in the mirror"?* Regina is essentially saying to you, "You must start with that man or woman in the mirror especially when it comes to *"Letting Go and Letting GOD"*.

Sure you have heard people say *"Let Go and Let God"* as if it is a cliché. The problem with the way it was said was that it wasn't backed up with HOW. I commend Regina on looking at various areas and providing with you several questions that you should ask yourself. I applaud her for saying you're responsible for your own happiness – because it's not your husband's responsibility or your wife's responsibility for that to happen.

I encourage you to read this through the first time and then read it again with a pen and paper in hand, make notes and begin to let GOD do a work in you like never before.

Taffy W. Wagner, D.Min, CEPF
CEO of Money Talk Matters, LLC
www.moneyandmarriage365.com

1 INTRODUCTION

To God be the Glory for the things HE has done!

I was compelled to write this book after writing an article on the subject well over 6+ years ago. Humbly honored, I received numerous comments and personal emails thanking me for the information.

I always tell people that God has a beautiful way of answering prayer in the most unique way we could ever imagine. God is not deaf to our prayers. He doesn't overlook our questions, our pain and definitely, our needs.

However, I believe, that God holds us accountable to His revelation (understanding of His word). As believers, it is our responsibility to seek Him for guidance, for understanding and then believe that He will do as He says. He is the ONLY Man that will not lie to us.

As you prepare to read this book, I pray that you will be encouraged, fulfilled and that your questions are answered by Him and Him only. I don't say this to say that I'm speaking on His behalf, because I'm not. I desire to be used by Him in any way HE deems fit. God gets ALL the glory and for this I'm grateful to share this content with you.

Last but surely not least, when you pray and ask God for guidance, remember, praying produces faith, faith produces belief, therefore, remove ALL doubt and be in expectancy for however God answers.

In all your getting, get understanding...

2 MY PERSONAL JOURNEY

I can only speak from my level of experience when it comes to seeking God for spiritual understanding. My journey is just that, mine – yours is your own. While they may be different, the word of God is the same yesterday, today and forever more.

I know when God touched my life. In other words, I remember the day, He let me know, He was right there with me.

I was 19 years old. I was pregnant and at the point of giving birth. While in the birthing center, I remember the nurse saying *"I don't hear a heart beat."* Everyone began to scramble to find out what was going on. As I was wheeled into the delivery room, my Aunt began to tell me what was going on. There was no heart beat from the baby. She was stillborn.

Upon leaving the hospital, I remember a couple of days later sitting in the dining room and wondering why my baby didn't make it. A voice from no where was peaceful and assured me that I was going to be okay and that I wasn't alone. I immediately knew it was God! There was a peace placed upon me that was not of this world. Although my Mom, Dad, Grandmother loved me unconditionally, they were unsuccessful in providing the comfort that God did.

From that day forth, I knew God loved and cared about me. I wasn't a bible scholar – yet I attended church regularly because that was the way we were raised. But that wasn't the beginning of my study – nor my desire to "get to know God" personally. As a matter of fact, it wasn't until years later – 10 years to be exact, that I sought after knowing what the word was and how it related to me.

My late husband (may he rest in sweet peace), was very knowledgeable of who Jesus was and why. He never pushed it on me or judged me because we were at two different places at that time. Gradually, he began to take me to church services that were 'different.' The type of services where people worshiped in a way I had never experienced before. They called out to God, not caring who was around them – they sought after God for their own personal reasons. At first, it was intimidating and scary. I had SO many questions like why were they doing certain things. I didn't feel all of that 'was necessary'. I didn't know what to think or what to do because it was just all too confusing for me. I was judging something I had zero knowledge of!

A short time later, a dear friend introduced us to a Woman who was madly in love with God. She was the type of person who wanted to impart everything she experienced and knew about God and would hold bible study to teach what she knew. We were then introduced to a minister whom, in my opinion, was the best teacher ever placed in my life.

He would sit at the kitchen table with us and read the scriptures over coffee, and then ask us what we understood about them. On one occasion, I specifically remember after reading a verse, him saying, *"now, who said that? Did I say it?"* That particular question helped me to understand that it wasn't about him, it was about the message. I no longer 'physically' looked at him as though my understanding or walk would be based on him and his approval – it was about understanding the bible – God's word, His direction and His approval.

3 I LET GO AND LET GOD

Later that evening, I went home and prayed to the Holy Spirit and asked Him to guide me according to what HE desired I know. I didn't want to 'appear' to understand, praise or worship because other people felt it necessary. I refused to do it for 'appearance sake', it had to be real – based on my understanding and the desire to praise God for what He was doing with me.

At that point, the Holy Spirit began to minister (teach) to my spirit. He brought the word of God alive to me. In other words, I understood what was meant for me to understand – not for you or anyone else for that matter – it was meant specifically for me. He gave me 'revelation' knowledge. He simply, answered my prayers.

An example of revelation knowledge is when you are reading the Bible and a verse leaps off the page, hits you between the eyes, and God says, "This is for you right now." - ref: cwgministries.org

I gained a strong appetite to know the word. I buried myself in reading the bible, praying and having one on one conversations with God. I desired to know the truth (as He specifically states: *"the truth will set you free" - John 8:32*), and what I learned from desiring the truth is, no matter what we're facing, good or bad, IF we truly desire understanding and know the truth to be FACT, it will always set you free. It will give you a sense of peace... because the truth is just that.. the truth.

Truth - sincerity in action, character, and utterance; the state of being the case: fact: the body of real things, events, and facts : actuality : a transcendent fundamental or spiritual reality : idea that is true or accepted as true. - ref: Websters dictionary

Does that make you a bad person? Absolutely not, however, you'll know and must accept the fact – that YOU made the choice and stop blaming God if it doesn't go as you wanted it to.

God's word is not complicated – His word specifically states that He is not the author of confusion (1 Cor. 14:33), therefore, when we're confused about a choice we make, especially after seeking Him for direction – it's because we have made our own decision on the matter, in other words "free will."

During my husband's illness, my relationship with God was so close, it was as though He moved in with us! I would sit on the patio, pray and read what He desired I read that day and then He would say things to me that only He could say.

On one particular morning, I remembered thinking, what if it were time for Ruben to go home to be with the Lord? And instantly, I heard God speak to me saying, *"You have a choice, you can choose the way the world thinks about death, or you can choose me."* (His guidance and teaching on death). Without any hesitation, I spoke out loud, *"Lord, I choose you."* I also remembered that I would pray for Ruben's healing however, my prayers would always end with: "not my will Lord, but THY will be done." At that moment, I didn't know what that would mean, only to find out when Ruben passed away, God gave me a *"peace that surspasseth all (worldly) understanding."* I knew it was his time to go and that there was nothing I, nor the doctors could do to keep him here. God blessed me to understand that it was His will.

I repeat, the truth of God's word is not confusing – it's about complete acceptance (it's about letting go and letting God do what He already purposed for the situation). When we know the truth, it allows us to make wisdom choices, whether or not our flesh agrees with them. Had I chose to think worldly thoughts about Ruben's home going, I would have been devastated, depressed and mourn without ceasing! I didn't want to live that way. I didn't desire for God's word to be in vain for my life! After all, my purpose of seeking Him, was to know the truth so that I wouldn't be ignorant to who He is.

4 PRAY, STUDY AND WORSHIP

I didn't just read, study, pray and worship so that I could say I knew the word! I desired to be knowledgeable in His word. To be worthy of His teachings. To *'study to show myself approved – rightly dividing the word of truth."* - *2 Tim 2:15*. I sincerely hungered and thirsted for the word of God but, more importantly, a personal relationship with Jesus Christ.

I say all of this to say, I've never desired to play around with (God) spirituality. It is what it is. It's not something you can pull off the shelf when you need it to just make you feel better and then put it back on the shelf when you want to 'hide' from the truth. You can't take bits and pieces of the word to satisfy or justify what you're going through, or use it to justify an excuse. You have to take it all! Even the parts that convicts your spirit when you know what you're doing is not right.

The bible was never intended to be a threat for us. It's not condemnation. It's also not a message to make you feel guilty about anything – simply put it's:

"Basic Instructions Before Leaving Earth." (BIBLE)

How's that for a strategic road map?

In order to have a relationship with Christ, we must speak to Him. This can be done through prayer, study and worship or by just having a simple conversation with Him. Praying in the simplest way, studying and asking the Holy Spirit to guide you according to what He has for you to learn and last but surely not least, by worshiping God through song, praise and dance. He repeatedly reminds me that, *"He inhabits the praises of His people."* - Psalms 22:3. In other words, He dwells (resides) in the atmosphere of His praise - He's pleased when we acknowledge Him through praise and worship.

5 FAITH

"Faith cometh by hearing, and by hearing the word of God." This is the purpose of ministry. When we attend church, bible study, or any faith filled seminar, program, or service, we are there to hear (with open spiritual ears, within our spirit) the word of God. It's not about anything else but having a spirit to learn more about Him.

"Faith is the substance of things hoped for and the evidence of things unseen." Hebrews 11:1

Definition: Faith is belief with strong conviction; firm belief in something for which there may be no tangible proof; complete trust; opposite of doubt. [Ref: christianity.com]

In order for Faith to work, it must be 'acted upon.' A great example of such faith is Noah, when he was instructed to build the ark, not knowing the end result but having immense faith (trust) in God to do as He instructed. Noah acted out his faith. This also
reminds me of the scripture, *"Faith without [action] works, is dead."* (James 2:14-26)

Faith is not temporal. In other words, it's not a temporary 'feeling'. You wouldn't want to say you have faith and then when things don't go (as fast) as you desire, you then deny the same faith you say you have (have faith – then LET GO and trust God!)

    ⅄ Definition: Substance, the tangible matter of which a thing consists; the essence, meaning, etc, of a written or spoken thought. [Ref: dictionary.com]

    ⅄ Definition: Things; all that can be described in the specified way.

⅄ Definition: Hope; a feeling of expectation and desire for a certain thing to happen. [dictionary.com]

⅄ Definition: Evidence; that which tends to prove or disprove something; something that makes plain or clear. [dictionary.com]

⅄ Definition: Unseen; not seen; unperceived; unobserved; invisible.

Another example, is having belief for a particular thing to come true [manifest], even when you can't see the proof beforehand.

I prayed for my husband's healing. I had unwavering faith that he would be healed! Regardless of what the doctors said, I believed until the day he passed. Now most would say, that's not faith, you believed in something and it didn't happen! Well, if I thought like that - according to my flesh, I could have easily agreed, but I didn't. God instructed me to trust Him and Him only. And because I trusted Him, He made sure I understood on the day that Ruben died, what faith truly meant – and because I let go and let Him – I was at TRUE peace in the matter. That day, the doctor came to me and said, "I know you have faith that your husband will be healed and he will, it just won't be here on earth." Talking about another level of revelation knowledge!

To elaborate further, some could even say, well that's a disappointment of faith. But my faith was not in man. My faith was in God to do what HE desired *("not my will Lord, but THY will be done!")* I trusted Him to do what He desired to do, regardless of my 'earthly' desire. On that same day, God also told me, "and now I give you my hidden secrets." Talking about clueless! Honestly speaking, I had no clear understanding of what that would entail!

As the days went by, I began to receive enormous clarity concerning life and death. He opened my eyes (gateway) to spiritual understanding. *"I was blind, but now I see."* - John 9:25; in other words, I was in the dark BUT NOW, I see clearly (without distortion, uncertainty or confusion.) Everything was made clear (with spiritual discernment).

"The effectual prayer of a righteous man, availeth much."

⅄ Definition: Effectual; producing or capable of producing an intended effect; adequate. Valid or binding, as an agreement or document.

⅄ Definition: Prayer; a devout petition to God; a conversation with God (in the name of Jesus).

⅄ Definition: Righteous; morally right or justifiable; acting in an upright, moral way

⅄ Definition: Avail; avail oneself of, to use to one's advantage

When we pray, we go with an intended result right? However, we must pray with a sincere heart as well as be in expectancy of a result, an answer, direction and or guidance. When we do this with a sincere desire of truth, God will answer accordingly.

He knows (us better than we know ourselves), our heart, mind, body, soul and spirit. He knows whether we're in humble submission or coming in a selfish way. This is why it's so important to have a personal relationship with Him. Based on our study life (of the word), He desires that we make our requests known to Him - Philippians 4:6 - (in other words, to bring back to His remembrance, His word/promises).

Example: "Father God, I thank you that all my needs are met according to your word. You said if I ask, I shall receive, when I seek, I shall find, when I knock, the door shall be opened. I'm letting go and letting YOU do what you promised you would do according to your perfect will for my life. I thank you for having heard this prayer and for having answered it, in Jesus name."

At this point, we should let go of all our own distorted thoughts of how we perceive things should be. We let go and let Him do what HE promised in the beginning (according to His word!)

It's up to YOU to be in right standing with God. It's not a play thing. Prayer is not something for you to take lightly. It's not a game so don't treat it that way, because if you do, in the end the only one disappointed will be YOU.

"Delight yourself in Him and He will give you the desires of your heart."
Psalm 37:4

Approximately seven years ago, this scripture bared witness to my spirit. It was the summer of 2004. As I walked down the driveway to pick up something off the ground, the Holy Spirit spoke very clearly to me saying: "to delight yourself in the Lord, means to joyfully desire God's desires [for you], in doing so, your heart will begin to desire what He specifically [designed] desires for you, thus those things shall be manifested in your life." At that point, I knew if I desired what He desired, then God would begin to give me the desires of my heart because they aligned with HIS desires, amen? This also reminds me of the scripture: *"the joy of the Lord is my strength."* - *Nehemiah 8:10*

There is a process of learning just how to *"delight yourself in God."*

Are you willing to go through the process? If so, here are a few suggestions to get you started on your blessed journey: Pray and sincerely ask the Holy Spirit to order your footsteps as you prepare to read God's words.

1. Clear your mind of all self-thoughts of how you "think" it should be. (As Paul stated to the Corinthians in 1 Corin 14:36; "Do you think that the knowledge of God's word begins and ends with you Corinthians? Well, you are mistaken!")

2. Be prepared to push your way through negative temptations of things like, "I don't understand what I'm reading" or "this doesn't make any sense" or "I don't have time to read" or "every time I try to read the bible, I get sleepy" (well, perhaps you do but, understand that the enemy doesn't want you to read it – begin to speak boldly and declare the good works of the Lord that you have already conquered the enemy and you're on your way to a victorious life in Jesus Christ!) and continue to read.

(Ref: "Watch and pray so that you will not fall into temptation. The spirit is willing, but the body is weak." Matt 26:41)

3. Make it a point to read at least 3 scriptures per day. Pray and ask the Holy Spirit to place these readings in your spirit so that when it's time for you to use them, He will bring them back to your remembrance.

4. Don't "try" so hard. God knows your heart. A sincere heart towards Him, will produce results.

5. STOP stressing. When you find yourself going to a place of stress, having tantrums or rebellious actions – STOP and ask yourself, "what do I look like to God right now?" Did you know that God knows what our needs are long before we do? Let go and let Him do what He promises all throughout His

message. BUT, if you feel you must continue through a tantrum, afterward, repent (ask for forgiveness), shake the dust and renew your mind to the will of God.

Note: "Discouragement, depression, and self-pity are the result of problems and adversity for some. For others, problems are a challenge and they help bring about faith, trust and victory."

6. Be willing to go through your storm! Pick up your cross and humbly carry it to its destination! God is able to use us for His glory when we're willing to puruse the purpose He intended for us long ago.

7. Place yourself in environments and with people that are positive and encouraging.

8. Instead of the "me, oh my" syndrome, with a sincere heart, pray for others.

9. "Trust in the Lord with all thine heart and lean not to your own understanding."

Letting Go and Letting God simply means you have to truly LET GO! And don't pick it back up! Once you realize this journey is NOT about you – but for the will and desire of the Lord, you're going to be okay!

All of this has made me a stronger person. Even in my darkest hours, I know without a shadow of doubt, I can go to Him for understanding regardless of the outcome. I don't walk around intimidated by man or woman. My trust is in Him and Him only. I've also learned how to be myself. Mind you, I'm not so heavenly bound that I'm no earthly good either. Meaning I don't walk around with a cross on my chest, or stand on a corner preaching, nor do I condemn others because of some holier than thou attitude – I just know who I am in Christ Jesus – I've been *"transformed by the renewing of my mind." - Romans 12:2*

6 APPROVAL ADDICTION

Here's where we get down to the nitty gritty of everyday life.

Some people are just nosy, insecure and unhappy with their life. To make matters worse, misery loves company! When you're going through a challenge, recognize that you're in a state of vulnerability, you're weak and sensitive to anything and everything, hence, you become unsure of things. You ask friends, co-workers, family members, neighbors and sometimes even strangers, questions about your circumstance just to look for approval (or for someone to be in agreement with your messed up choice!)

DON'T DO IT!

Joyce Meyers wrote a book on Approval Addiction – she went really deep with the subject therefore if this is something you're struggling with, drop by your local library, bookstore or Amazon.com to pick up a copy.

God knows I use to be like that! I wanted to be liked by everybody! When I was younger, if my family or friends didn't approve (it didn't matter what it was), I would do whatever it took, just to please them.

I learned the hard way that people don't always have your best interest at heart – and yes, including family. Sometimes their judgment is cloudy, sometimes there's a spirit of jealousy floating around and sometimes they don't know what to say – there are even times they don't want to hurt your feelings by telling you the truth so they agree with you – when they do that, it could cost you dearly!

Don't look for approval just to justify your actions, choices or for people to like you. The truth will ALWAYS undoubtedly set you free.

You have to search yourself – who are you? What do you believe? Are you empty and so shallow that you're selfish and only want your way in a situation? Are you so closed mind and so "right" that only what you say is right or means anything? Think again.

7 VERBAL ABUSE

When I wrote the article I mentioned in the beginning of this book, *"How To Let Go and Let God"*, most of the responses I received whether openly on the blog or via private email, concerned women who were in relationships with abusive men or adulterous relationships they were trying to justify because of "love."

So let's talk about that now okay?

God DOES NOT approve abuse or adultery. Point blank. So don't even try to justify that because it's a LIE!

Also remember, I'm not pointing the finger at you because I've done some things in my past that were SO wrong it's ridiculous! However, I've repented for those things and let go of them to NEVER do again.

Here are references to that in the bible:

Colossians 3:19 - Husbands, love your wives, and do not be harsh with them.

Psalm 11:5 - The Lord tests the righteous, but his soul hates the wicked and the one who loves violence.

2 Timothy 3:1-8 - But understand this, that in the last days there will come times of difficulty. For people will be lovers of self, lovers of money, proud, arrogant, abusive, disobedient to their parents, ungrateful, unholy, heartless, unappeasable, slanderous, without self-control, brutal, not loving good, treacherous, reckless, swollen with conceit, lovers of pleasure rather than lovers of God, having the appearance of godliness, but denying its power. Avoid such people.

Ephesians 4:29-32 - Let no corrupting talk come out of your mouths, but only such as is good for building up, as fits the occasion, that it may give grace to those who hear. And do not grieve the Holy Spirit of God, by whom you were sealed for the day of redemption. Let all bitterness and wrath and anger and clamor and slander be put away from you, along with all malice. Be kind to one another, tenderhearted, forgiving one another, as God in Christ forgave you.

If you're in an abusive relationship, whether verbal or physical, first, ask yourself the following questions:

1. Why are you attracted to that type of behavior? Does it have something to do with your past?
2. Are you taking the blame because you believe you deserve it?
3. Are you overlooking those things because you "love" him or her?
4. What exactly do you define as love?

"Love is patient, love is kind. It does not envy, it does not boast, it is not proud. It does not dishonor others, it is not self-seeking, it is not easily angered, it keeps no record of wrongs. Love does not delight in evil but rejoices with the truth. It always protects, always trusts, always hopes, always perseveres."
- 1 Corin 13:4-7

I once had a friend who possessed those traits. When things didn't go 'his' way, he was deliberately {verbally} abusive. He would express every pain he harbored within himself towards me. He didn't realize that it wasn't me who he was angered with – but because I was there, he dumped it on me – making me the villain. He would say things to me like:

"you need to see a doctor because there's definitely something wrong with you!"

"you planned this all day long so you could go be with

your (other) man."

"are you that dense you can't figure out what I'm saying to you?"

"see, your family and friends think the same way I do about you, you have a problem!" etc., etc.

But to God be the glory! I recognized it right off the bat! I was like, "no way am I going to accept this type of [abusive] behavior!" I know who I am in Christ Jesus and this isn't it! LOL!

No one has the right to attempt to strip you of your self identity! No one has the right to persecute you in a way that it hurts so deeply you have to ask yourself – is this true? No one has the right to define who you are!

I've seen so many Women who "settle" just to say they have a man. Of course most people would love to have a companion in his/her life, but it shouldn't be at the risk of losing your self identity. It's not your responsibility when a person has had challenges that cause them to be the way they are. Yes, you can help them by praying for them and putting them in God's hands, BUT you can't fix them and staying with them as long as they continue to abuse you – is not a solution!

Now does that mean you're perfect and there's some things about you that need fixing? No and yes. No one is perfect however, IF your partner chooses to point some things out to you concerning your behavior, it should NEVER be in a volatile way! Calmly discussing the issues, in my opinion, will result in a much better way than abuse!

When you learn to put God first in your life, everything else will follow accordingly. He'll help you to realize who you are and Who's you are! He won't abuse you nor will He make you feel inferior (less than.)

There's is so much peace in walking away from something that you know you should not partake in. It elevates your character, integrity and humility. It also defines who you truly are as a person. God desires that we have a "boldness" (in HIM) knowing who we are. That boldness however, can't be boastful, selfish nor conceited.

Being bold in Christ signifies that you understand your responsibility in fulfilling everything God purposes for your life – it means not seeking ways to please man but to please Him who created you in His image. God is not weak and is not tempted by man – for {approval} acceptance, neither are you if you so choose. Boldness comes from God when we choose to let go and let Him be the authority, thereby He receives the glory and you won't get "pumped up" {conceited} in yourself.

If you have children, consider them second – yes second, because if you only do it for them, eventually, you'll continue to attract those same characteristics in another person. You have to do it for yourself – then them.

"What shall we then say to these things? If God [be] for us, who [can be] against us?" - Romans 8:31

You and I know that there's a process to everything in life. It takes time to realize how much God sincerely loves you – just understand with EVERY fiber of your being that He   desires for you to know that above all else, He is the only one who has your complete best interests at heart. He's NOT against you – He's for YOU! Allow Him to guide you through the process of eliminating the things He detests because they don't belong to you.

8 ADULTERY

"voluntary sexual activity between a married man and someone other than his wife or between a married woman and someone other than her husband"

Make a selfish decision to do this one and get ready to "reap what you sow," because it's definitely going to happen!

There is NO justifiable reason to commit adultery. I don't care what he or she says to you. As long as the person is married, it is unacceptable to have a intimate (lustful) relationship therewith, including non-sexual activities (with a married man or woman) such as meeting for breakfast, lunch or dinner, going to the movies, talking on the phone, meeting at the park -- you get it right?

I had a woman say to me that she knew it was wrong but she loved him. Notice again what was said...

"I know it is wrong... BUT, I love him." That's self justification for doing something you know is wrong. The Holy Spirit once said to me "an excuse is a justification to make the soul feel good." Mind you, He said, "the soul" - you know why? Because *I* believe the spirit does not bare witness to an untruth.

Let me ask you a question, if you were happily married and never thought of your spouse cheating outside of your marriage, only to find out they were, how would you feel? Would you feel cheated? Trust violation? Deception? Of course you would, so why justify it for selfish reasons just because "you" want to cheat? More importantly, if you say you love God – how can you so easily justify it? And if you know what God knows, it should be a simple choice – don't do it!

Per topbibleverses.com, *"Adultery is the most condemned of all the sexual sins; it is mentioned in the Ten Commandments, all four Gospels, and ten other books of the Bible."*

"You shall not commit adultery." | "But a man who commits adultery lacks judgment; whoever does so destroys himself." Exodus 20:14

Also meditate on Matthew 5:27-32.

This is definitely one topic I'm not open for (debate) discussion on. Point blank, when you choose to commit adultery, you can't hide from God. It amazes me how people try to hide this from friends, family, co-workers, etc., they may not see you or ever catch you in the act BUT God, knows and sees all – that's where your major concern should be – in HIM! Here are a few suggestions:

1. Repent (sincerely ask God for forgiveness)
2. Research the bible on adultery then meditate on it (ask the Holy Spirit for guidance and understanding).
3. Tell the other person involved, you've made a decision that this is not in your best interest to continue (no explanation needed because most likely, they'll try to talk (romance) you out of it.
4. Tell the enemy, he is a lie and that "greater is He that is in you, that he is in the word", [1 John 4:4] for example, you're not looking for fleshly desires or acceptance.
5. Ask your praying friends and family to pray for you without ceasing.
6. Pray (without ceasing) daily (speaking the scriptures out loud)
7. Begin hanging out with friends and family who won't judge you but help you through the process

It's not as hard as you think, it's nothing to it, but to do it!

9 PROBLEMS IN YOUR RELATIONSHIPS

Early on in our marriage, I use to think that I had problems. I say use to because God gave me a lesson that I will never forget!

It didn't matter what it was, I blamed my husband for everything! If things weren't going right for me, I would blame him because it had to have something to do with him – why else was I going through this?

Yeah right!

I remember telling my Dad that Ruben was living off of my goodness. In other words, he was fortunate in life because of me. I actually use to think that because I made more money than him, we did okay because of me! It was me who was the honcho in this relationship! If it weren't for me, where would he be? Isn't that horrible, selfish and conceited? Uh-yeah!

One day as I was cleaning the kitchen, God stopped me right in my tracks. He spoke to me and said, "until you repent and change your awkward thinking, nothing will change for the better for you – who do you think you are?" Talking about a serious wake up call! You better believe I got myself together and with the quickness!

I knew I had to not only ask God for forgiveness, but I had to also go to my husband and ask him as well. I had to realize that our marriage was not based on me and me only! It was not based on the fact that my husband was "lucky" to have me because I thought I was all that and a bag of chips to go along with it.

I had to seek God for the answers as to why I did what I did and what was the right path to take with this. I eventually realized that God was the head of my husband and my husband was the head of the family. As long as he had the best interest of our family in mind, I was to humbly submit to my husband.

Now does that mean I had to forget about myself in the process? No. It meant that I had to understand what true marriage is in the eyesight of God. Some Women have a serious problem with submission. They think once they submit it's like being "less than" according to the world.

"When you make a vow to God, do not delay in fulfilling it. He has no pleasure in fools; fulfill your vow." Ecclesiastes 5:4

As a Christian, marriage is a holy covenant. When we take our marriage vows, it's just that serious. We're not just repeating the words that the minister says for the heck of it, we're making a vow unto God (and we really need to be careful when we do that). You should ask yourself what does marriage REALLY mean to you and are you willing to REALLY be there for the good as well as the bad?

Later on in our marriage, Ruben and I were willing to do whatever it took for our marriage to work. We became best friends – friends who sincerely trusted each other. Having this type of friendship, allowed us to "listen" whether or not we agreed with what was said but, to come to a conclusion as to what was the best solution for our family. We had long, in-depth discussions about how we felt about a particular situation or thing. We learned how to communicate.

(Get this and you're going to have a serious breakthrough! □ It's not about who's right or wrong – however, it has everything to do with sincerely respecting each other as individuals and then concluding with the best (solution) decision for the situation.

Men seriously need to understand that their wives are NOT their children or someone they can just mold into who they want them to be for their own selfish reasons – they are the "help meet".

Women seriously need to understand why they chose to marry "him." You shouldn't just marry a man because he's socially acceptable and financially able to take care of you (although those are great characteristics ☐), believe it or not, it's not his responsibility (or ingredients for a 'happy' marriage) to make you happy (and vice versa.) If you aren't already happy, you're in for a turbulent ride!

Couples aren't taking the time to really "get to know each other." Some people only get married for financial reasons, sexually compatibility, children born out of wedlock, physical appearance and because they just want to be married. UGH!

Consider the following:

- ⅄ Are you spirituality compatible?
- ⅄ Do you sincerely like each other (like going to the same places together, respect each others family, not intimidated of each other, capable of making sound financial decisions together and have similar goals?)
- ⅄ Have you talked about what marriage means when it concerns the two of you?
- ⅄ Do you truly understand the vows you're making before God?
- ⅄ Are you truly willing to be there for the good and the bad?
- ⅄ Are you willing to go through pre-marital counseling with your Minister?

I've heard so many people say when their marriage is in trouble, "God doesn't favor divorce." Well no, He doesn't

BUT – do you understand the vows when the minister says, "what God hath put together, let not man put asunder?" In other words, did you both pray about this separately and together before making the decision to get married? Did God give His stamp of approval on this beforehand? I personally think if the two of you didn't ask God in the first place whether or not He put it together, at some point, you're going to have to ask Him to help you get through it – as a matter of fact, it's quite likely you're going to have to ask Him that quite often EVEN if He did.

You are not always going to agree on everything. I encourage couples to learn how to humble themselves to agree to disagree. It's never too late to get your marriage in order.

It's so much more than just planning a wedding and showing up at the alter in front of family and friends for appearance wise. Marriage takes work but it's not as complicated as we make it sometimes. As long as both parties are willing to work together for a fruitful and long relationship, it can be the most beautiful relationship in the world!

10 LEARNING HOW TO LET GO

Okay, so I do understand that not everybody knows this and right now, you might just need help learning how to let go and let God help you out of this situation. If you have a guilty conscious, your spirit will definitely convict you. It might not be something you pay attention to much because you don't want to literally "face" what you know is wrong however, deep down you know it's not right because your spirit is constantly reminding you that something's wrong!

One of the most important things that we must learn when it comes to letting go and letting God, is to understand that God's love for us is quite different than our definition of what true love is.

Give It Over to God

Whatever it is you need to let go of, whether the points I mentioned above (regarding   adultery, relationships, your job, your business, an unhealthy habit, or any challenge you may be going through...) letting go means to simply – let go. To release something. When we let go and let God, we are trusting Him to take over, amen?

"Cast your cares on the LORD and he will sustain you; He will never let the righteous fall." Psalm 55:22

This is not something we magically understand overnight, it's a process of elimination. Eliminating (dying of) ourselves – in order for God to handle the situation for us. The battle, really isn't ours to undertake. God already knows we aren't capable of doing it alone! We just have to make the decision to trust Him through the process.
The above scripture specifically indicates that He will never

let the righteous fail... so who are "the righteous?" Those who are in right standing with God. In other words, those who have accepted Jesus Christ as their personal Savior and believe in the trinity -- the Father, Son and Holy Ghost. ALL of us have fallen short – so don't think that you don't fit in with the "righteous" - not one of us is perfect and never will be as long as we're here on earth, I don't care how many church services you attend, how many church auxiliaries you are a member of, how much you read the bible or how much you pray – we all have something to repent for. When we do this, God will deliver us from unrighteousness.

Right standing means – having a personal relationship with Him. Knowing that God loves you unconditionally and that you seek HIM for counsel and believe that He is God and that He's the ONLY one faithful to His promises. Right standing also means to let go of the things that we know are not of Him, the things that are wrong in His eyesight, also... the things that He knows, that we know, He knows... we know, amen?

He knows what we know when it comes to anything and everything - INCLUDING Him! Isn't that amazing? At that point we become accountable to those things. Those are the things we will have to answer for. I made a decision a long time ago that when it's my time to go before Him, I surely hope I won't have to answer for something I know I kept doing when I knew it was wrong! I hope to only have to answer for something I was sincerely unaware of.

Last but surely not least, learn to submit yourself to God. *"Submit yourselves therefore to God. Resist the devil, and he will flee from you." James 4:7*

When you know what you know, you'll be able to "shake the

dust", i.e, to walk away with confidence knowing and trusting that God will step in for you. Maybe not when you want it, but He is always on time!

"My sheep hear my voice, and I know them, and they follow me..."
John 10:27

I pray that this writing has helped you in some way to understand how to let go and let God. It may not hold all the answers you are looking for – normally these things are never all found in a book, a person, or a "how to" session, for me it was seeking God with a sincere and humble request – to know Him personally and to hear His voice.

With sincere, humble and holy submission to Christ Jesus – I let go and let God! - I hope you'll do the same.

"May the grace of the Lord Jesus Christ, and the love of God, and the fellowship of the Holy Spirit be with you.." (2 Corin 13:14)

ABOUT THE AUTHOR

Regina Baker, known as the *"Keeping It Real"* certified biblical, internet & network marketing business consultant, knows what it's like to really *"let go and let God."*

> *"Life is REALLY like a box of chocolates, you never know what you're gonna get."*

When faced with the devastating news of her late husband's diagnosis, terminal cancer, Regina sought out for the real understanding of how faith and letting go and let God would help her through the difficult times ahead.

Pray and Listen

"Cause me to hear Your loving-kindness in the morning, for You do I lean and in You do I trust. Cause me to know the way wherein I should walk, for I lift up my inner self to you." Psalm 141:8

Baker says, *"it's only when you deeply seek God for spiritual understanding, that you'll ever be blessed with knowing that the battle really isn't yours, and that by surrendering everything over to God is as simple as making a sincere decision to do just that."*

While the journey wasn't an easy one, it was the best time of her life. She formed a relationship with Jesus Christ, studied the word on a daily basis and received a *"peace that surspasseth ALL worldly understanding."*

Baker says, *"God holds us accountable to His revelation (understanding of His word). As believers, it is our responsibility to seek Him for guidance, for understanding and then believe that He will do as He says."* Letting Go and Let God is not as complicated as we try to make it.

After a two year journey and going through the process, and

becoming a Certified Biblical Consultant, Regina enjoys helping others to get past their pain to their power.

In all your getting… GET understanding!

To contact Regina, email: regina@howtoletgoandletgod.com or visit: www.howtoletgoandletgod.com

Stay tuned for more series regarding How To Let Go and Let God!

Have a testimony you want to share of
Letting Go and Let God?
email: testimony@howtoletgoandletgod.com

RECOMMENDED RESOURCES

Bride and Groom Money Talk -
www.brideandgroommoneytalk.com

Love Life Designs - www.lovelifedesignsllc.com

So He Cheated, Now What? - www.sohecheated.com

The Ten Commandments of Marriage -
www.hitchedmag.com/10commandments.php

**Approval Addiction: Overcoming Your Need to Please
Everyone** – Amazon.com

You Have Permission to Succeed –
www.edwinhaynes.com

Made in the USA
San Bernardino, CA
15 April 2017